HAL•LEONARD
INSTRUMENTAL
PLAY-ALONG

AUDIO ACCESS
INCLUDED

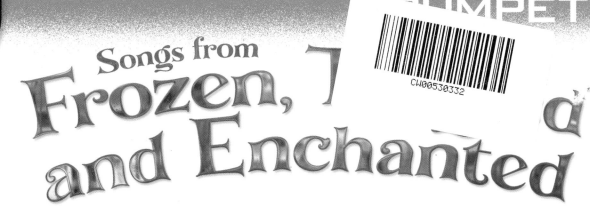

Songs from
Frozen, Tangled
and Enchanted

TRUMPET

CONTENTS

To access audio visit:
www.halleonard.com/mylibrary

Enter Code
7565-2686-7345-3733

Audio Arrangements by Peter Deneff

ISBN 978-1-4803-8725-6

Disney characters and artwork © Disney Enterprises, Inc.

WALT DISNEY MUSIC COMPANY
WONDERLAND MUSIC COMPANY, INC.

DISTRIBUTED BY

HAL•LEONARD®
CORPORATION
7777 W. BLUEMOUND RD. P.O. BOX 13819 MILWAUKEE, WI 53213

In Australia Contact:
Hal Leonard Australia Pty. Ltd.
4 Lentara Court
Cheltenham, Victoria, 3192 Australia
Email: ausadmin@halleonard.com.au

Visit Hal Leonard Online at
www.halleonard.com

DO YOU WANT TO BUILD A SNOWMAN?

from Disney's Animated Feature FROZEN

TRUMPET

Music and Lyrics by KRISTEN ANDERSON-LOPEZ
and ROBERT LOPEZ

FOR THE FIRST TIME IN FOREVER

from Disney's Animated Feature FROZEN

TRUMPET

Music and Lyrics by KRISTEN ANDERSON-LOPEZ
and ROBERT LOPEZ

HAPPY WORKING SONG

from Walt Disneys Pictures' ENCHANTED

Music by ALAN MENKEN
Lyrics by STEPHEN SCHWARTZ

TRUMPET

I SEE THE LIGHT

from Walt Disney Pictures' TANGLED

TRUMPET

Music by ALAN MENKEN
Lyrics by GLENN SLATER

poco rit.   a tempo

rit.   **mp**

I'VE GOT A DREAM

from Walt Disney Pictures' TANGLED

TRUMPET

Music by ALAN MENKEN
Lyrics by GLENN SLATER

IN SUMMER

from Disney's Animated Feature FROZEN

TRUMPET

Music and Lyrics by KRISTEN ANDERSON-LOPEZ
and ROBERT LOPEZ

LET IT GO
from Disney's Animated Feature FROZEN

TRUMPET

Music and Lyrics by KRISTEN ANDERSON-LOPEZ
and ROBERT LOPEZ

LOVE IS AN OPEN DOOR

from Disney's Animated Feature FROZEN

TRUMPET

Music and Lyrics by KRISTEN ANDERSON-LOPEZ
and ROBERT LOPEZ

MOTHER KNOWS BEST

from Walt Disney Pictures' TANGLED

Music by ALAN MENKEN
Lyrics by GLENN SLATER

TRUMPET

SO CLOSE
from Walt Disney Pictures' ENCHANTED

TRUMPET

Music by ALAN MENKEN
Lyrics by STEPHEN SCHWARTZ

Moderately, with feeling

Small notes optional

THAT'S HOW YOU KNOW
from Walt Disney Pictures' ENCHANTED

TRUMPET

Music by ALAN MENKEN
Lyrics by STEPHEN SCHWARTZ

TRUE LOVE'S KISS

from Walt Disney Pictures' ENCHANTED

TRUMPET

Music by ALAN MENKEN
Lyrics by STEPHEN SCHWARTZ

WHEN WILL MY LIFE BEGIN

from Walt Disney Pictures' TANGLED

TRUMPET

Music by ALAN MENKEN
Lyrics by GLENN SLATER

Moderately